EXPLORING NATURE

WHALES & DOLPHINS

Dive into the watery world of whales, dolphins, narwhals
and rorquals, all shown in 190 spectacular images

Robin Kerrod
Consultant: Michael Bright

ARMADILLO

This edition is published by Armadillo,
an imprint of Anness Publishing Ltd,
Blaby Road, Wigston, Leicestershire LE18 4SE;
info@anness.com

www.annesspublishing.com

Anness Publishing has a picture agency
outlet for images for publishing,
promotions or advertising. Please visit
our website www.practicalpictures.com
for more information.

Publisher: Joanna Lorenz
Managing Editor: Linda Fraser
Senior Editor: Nicole Pearson
Editor: Louisa Somerville
Designer: Vivienne Gordon
Illustrators: Julian Baker, David Webb
Production Controller: Pirong Wang

PUBLISHER'S NOTE
Although the advice and information in this book
are believed to be accurate and true at the time
of going to press, neither the authors nor the
publisher can accept any legal responsibility or
liability for any errors or omissions that may
have been made.

Manufacturer: Anness Publishing Ltd,
Blaby Road, Wigston, Leicestershire
LE18 4SE, England
For Product Tracking go to:
www.annesspublishing.com/tracking
Batch: 6775-22665-1127

PICTURE CREDITS
(b=bottom, t=top, m=middle, l=left, r=right)
Animals Animals: pages 11tr, 38tm, 45m and 55t;
Bruce Coleman: pages 4b, 9b, 13tr, 13br, 15tl,
19tl, 20t, 21t, 22t, 27b, 39t, 42b, 43m, 45t, 46t,
48b, 54b, 57t, 60t and 61m; **Bridgeman Art
Library**: pages 31mr and 59b; **Ecoscene**: pages
8mb, 8bl, 9m and 41br; **Mary Evans Picture
Library**: page 9tl; **FLPA**: pages 2, 3, 7tr, 7bl, 10t,
10bl, 12b, 14t, 19ml, 19mr, 23t, 24m, 30m, 32–33,
32t, 32b, 34b, 35t, 36–37, 36l, 42t, 50t, 50bl,
52–53, 52ml, 52b, 53bl, 54m, 55t, 56t, 58b and
61t; **NASA**: page 17br; **Natural History
Museum**: pages 4–5m, 6m and 49ml; **Natural
Science Photos**: pages 18m and 26b; **Nature
Photographers**: pages 11m and 58t; **NHPA**:
pages 1, 12tr, 15b, 24tl, 24b, 29t, 29b, 34t, 35b,
37t, 37b, 38bl, 56m, 57m, 57b, 58m and 61b;
Oxford Scientific Films: pages 2, 5bl, 6b, 8mr,
13bl, 16bl, 16br, 18tl, 20b, 21b, 22m, 22b, 25b,
27t, 28t, 28b, 29ml, 29mr, 30b, 31t, 31ml, 33b,
35m, 36b, 38mr, 39b, 40b, 41t, 41bl, 42m, 43t,
44m, 49mr, 49b, 55m, 56b and 59t; **Planet Earth
Pictures**: pages 2, 4tr, 11bl, 14b, 16t, 18b, 19b,
23m, 25t, 26, 30t, 31b, 39m, 44t, 44b, 45b, 46m,
46b, 47t, 47m, 47b, 48t, 49t, 50m, 51mr, 51bl,
51br, 53mr, 54t, 59m and 60b; **Spacecharts**: page
5tl and 17b; **Visual Arts Library**: pages 10mr,
15m and 53br; **Zefa Pictures**: pages 5tr and 51t.

INTRODUCING WHALES

  4 Whale Order
  6 Whales Large and Small

HOW WHALES WORK

  8 Whale Bones
10 Whale Bodies
12 Staying Alive
14 Whale Brain and Senses

HOW WHALES BEHAVE

16 Sounds and Songs
18 Feeding Habits
20 Focus on Killer Whales
22 Focus on Lunging
     for Lunch
24 Swimming
26 Focus on Diving

T E N T S

WHALE SOCIAL LIFE

28 Social Life

30 The Mating Game

32 Focus on Bringing up Baby

34 Having Fun

36 Focus on Whales on Display

THE WHALE WORLD

38 Where Whales are Found

40 Migration

42 High and Dry

44 Grey and Right Whales

46 Rorquals

48 Sperm and White Whales

50 Beaked, Pilot and Killer Whales

52 Oceanic Dolphins

54 Porpoises and River Dolphins

FANTASTIC FACTS

56 Similar Swimmers

58 Whale Slaughter

60 Whale Conservation

62 Glossary

64 Index

Whale Order

Like fish, whales and dolphins spend all their lives in the sea. But unlike fish, they breathe air, have warm blood and suckle their young. They are more closely related to human beings than fish because they are mammals. Many whales are enormous – some are as big and as heavy as a train carriage full of passengers. Dolphins are much smaller – most are about the same size as an adult human being. Porpoises, which look much like dolphins, are also roughly the same size as humans. Although smaller, dolphins and porpoises are kinds of whales, too. All whales belong to the major group, or order, of animals called Cetacea.

▲ HEAVYWEIGHTS
The largest of the whales are the biggest animals ever to have lived. This leaping humpback whale is nearly 15m/50ft long and weighs over 25 tons – as much as five adult elephants. Some other kinds of whales, such as the fin and blue whales, are much bigger.

► WHALE ANCESTORS
More than 50 million years ago, creatures like this were swimming in the seas. They seem to have been ancestors of modern cetaceans. This creature, named Basilosaurus (meaning king lizard), grew up to over 20m/65ft long. It had a snake-like body with tiny front flippers and traces of a pair of hind limbs.

▼ BALEEN WHALES
These humpback whales are feeding in Alaskan waters. They belong to the group, or suborder, of whales known as the baleen whales. These are in general very much larger than those in the other main group, the toothed whales.

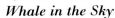

Whale in the Sky

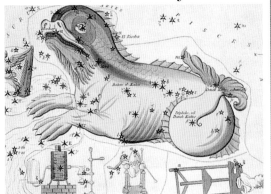

This star map shows a constellation of stars named Cetus, meaning the sea monster or whale. In Greek mythology, Cetus was a monster that was about to eat Andromeda, a maiden who had been chained to a rock as a sacrifice. Along came Perseus, who killed the sea monster and saved Andromeda.

▲ TOOTHED WHALES

A bottlenose dolphin opens its mouth and shows its teeth. It is one of the many species of toothed whales. Toothed whales have much simpler teeth than land mammals and many more of them. The bottlenose dolphin, for example, has up to 50 teeth in both its upper and lower jaws.

◄ BREATHING

Because they are mammals, whales and dolphins breathe air. This common dolphin breathes out through a blowhole on top of its head as it rises to the surface. It can hold its breath for five minutes or more when diving.

Did you know? A blue whale can weigh as much as 25 elephants.

Whales Large and Small

Most large whales belong to the major group of cetaceans called the baleen whales. Instead of teeth, these whales have brush-like plates, called baleen, that hang from their upper jaw. They use the baleen to filter food from the water. The sperm whale does not belong to the baleen group. It belongs to the other major cetacean group, called the toothed whales. This group also includes the dolphins, porpoises, white whales and beaked whales. All of these cetaceans have teeth for biting and grasping the prey they feed on.

▲ GREY WHALE
The grey whale can grow up to nearly 15m/50ft long, and tip the scales at 35 tons or more. It is a similar size to the humpback, sei, bowhead and right whales, but looks quite different. Instead of the smooth skin of other whales, the grey has rough skin and no proper dorsal fin on its back.

Did you know? Some whales have as many as 3,000 baleen plates in their jaws.

▲ BLACK AND WHITE
The bowhead whale, which has a highly curved jaw, grows to 16m/52ft. It is closely related to the right whale. The bowhead is famous for its long baleen plates and thick layer of blubber. The toothed whales we call belugas (*above left*) grow to about 4.5m/15ft at most. The first part of the word beluga means white in Russian, and belugas are also known as white whales.

▶ SEI WHALE

At up to about 16m/52ft, the sei whale looks much like its bigger relatives, the blue whale and the fin. All are members of the group called rorquals, which have deep grooves in their throat. These grooves let the throat expand to take big mouthfuls of water for feeding. Seis have up to 60 grooves in their throat.

Did you know? The blue whale's tongue weighs as much as an African elephant.

▶ RELATIVE SIZES

Whales come in many sizes, from dolphins smaller than a human to the enormous blue whale, which can grow to 30m/98ft or more. In general, the baleen whales are much bigger than the toothed whales. The exception is the sperm whale, which can grow up to 19m/62ft.

porpoise

dolphin

narwhal

killer whale

beaked whale

grey whale

sperm whale

right whale

blue whale

▲ RISSO'S DOLPHIN

The dolphin pictured leaping here is a Risso's dolphin. It has a blunt snout and as few as six teeth. Most of the toothed whales that we call dolphins are on average about 2–3m/6–10ft long. Risso's dolphins can grow a little bigger – up to nearly 4m/13ft long.

7

Whale Bones

Like all mammals, whales have a skeleton of bones to give the body its shape and protect vital organs like the heart. Because a whale's body is supported by water, its bones are not as strong as those of land mammals, and are quite soft. The backbone is made up of many vertebrae, with joints in between to give it flexibility. While providing some body support, the backbone acts mainly as an anchor for the muscles, particularly the strong muscles that drive the tail. Instead of limbs, a whale has a pair of modified fore limbs, called flippers.

◄ BONE CORSET
This advertisement for a "whalebone" corset dates from 1911, a time when women wore corsets to give them a shapely figure. The corsets were, in fact, made from the baleen plates found in whales' mouths.

► UNDERNEATH THE ARCHES
Arches built from the jaw bones of huge baleen whales can be seen in some ports that were once the home of whaling fleets. This jaw-bone arch can be seen outside Christ Church Cathedral in Port Stanley, Falkland Islands. Nowadays, whales are protected species and building such arches is forbidden.

► HANDS UP
The bones in a sperm whale's flipper are remarkably similar to those in a human hand. A whale's flippers are a much changed version of a typical mammal's front limbs. Both hands have wrist bones, finger bones and joints.

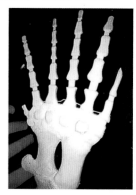
sperm whale flipper

human hand

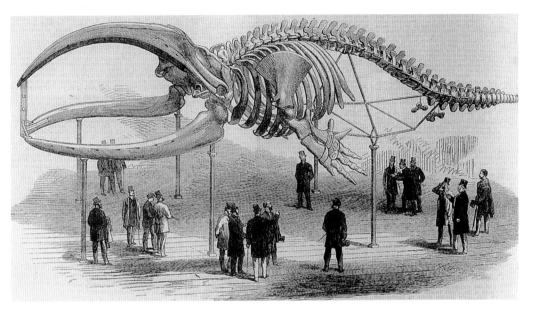

◄ BIG HEAD

This whale skeleton was displayed in London in 1830. Its large jaw bones tell us that it is a baleen whale, which needs a big mouth for feeding. Like other mammals, it has a large rib cage to protect its body organs. However, it has no hind limbs or pelvic girdle.

Whales are very oily and very smelly. Did you know?

▼ TOOTHY JAW

This is the skeleton of a false killer whale, one of the toothed whales. The head is much smaller than that of the baleen whales, and its jaws are studded with teeth. Its long spine is made up of segments called vertebrae. The vertebrae in the whale's waist region are large, so that they are strong enough to anchor the animal's powerful tail muscles.

▼ KILLER SKULL

Both jaws of this killer whale skull are studded with vicious, curved teeth that are more than 10cm/4in long. The killer whale is a deadly predator, which attacks seals, dolphins and sometimes whales that are even bigger than itself.

Whale Bodies

Over many millions of years, whales have developed features that suit them to a life spent mostly underwater. They have long, rounded bodies and smooth, almost hairless skin. Like fish, whales move about using fins. They have the same body organs, such as heart and lungs, as land mammals. In the big whales, however, the body organs are much larger than in land mammals.

▼ BIG MOUTH

This grey whale is one of the baleen whales, and the baleen can be seen hanging from its upper jaw. Baleen whales need a big mouth so that they can take in large mouthfuls of water when they are feeding. Grey whales usually feed at the bottom of the sea.

baleen

Jonah and the Whale

This picture from the 17th century tells one of the best known of all Bible stories. The prophet Jonah was thrown overboard by sailors during a terrible storm. To rescue him, God sent a whale, which swallowed him whole. Jonah spent three days in the whale's belly before it coughed him up on to dry land. The picture shows that many people at this time had little idea of what a whale looked like. The artist has given it shark-like teeth and a curly tail.

▼ **LEAPING DOLPHINS**

A pair of bottlenose dolphins leap effortlessly several metres/feet out of the water. Powerful muscles near the tail provide them with the energy for fast swimming and leaping. They leap for various reasons – to signal to each other, to look for fish or perhaps just for fun.

▲ **HANGERS ON**

This humpback whale's throat is covered with barnacles, which take hold because the whale moves quite slowly. They cannot easily cling to swifter-moving cetaceans, such as dolphins. A dolphin sheds rough skin as it moves through the water. This also makes it harder for a barnacle to take hold.

▶ **LOUSY WHALES**

The skin of the grey whale is covered with light patches. These patches are clusters of ten-legged lice, called cyamids, about 2–3cm/¾–1¼in long. They feed on the whale's skin.

◀ **BODY LINES**

A pod, or group, of melon-headed whales swim in the Pacific Ocean. This species is one of the smaller whales, at less than 3m/10ft long. It shows the features of a typical cetacean – a well-rounded body with a short neck and a single fin. It has a pair of paddle-like front flippers and a tail with horizontal flukes.

Did you know? Whales have whiskers on their faces.

11

Staying Alive

Whales are warm-blooded creatures. To stay alive, they must keep their bodies at a temperature of about 36–37°C/96.8–98.6°F. They swim in very cold water that quickly takes heat away from the surface of their bodies. To stop body heat from reaching the surface, whales have a thick layer of a fatty substance called blubber just beneath the skin. Whales must also breathe to stay alive and they do this through a blowhole, situated on top of the head. When a whale breathes out, it sends a column of steamy water vapour high into the air.

▲ IN THE WARM
Southern right whales feed in icy Antarctic waters in summer. The whales' size helps limit the percentage of body heat they lose to the water.

epidermis

blood vessels

layer of blubber

◄ SKIN DEEP
This is a cross-section of a whale's outer layer. Beneath its skin, a thick layer of blubber insulates it from ice-cold water.

► SMALL BODY
The Atlantic spotted dolphin is about the size of a human. Because it is small, its body has a relatively large surface area for its size and so loses heat faster than its big relatives. This is probably why the Atlantic spotted dolphin lives in warm waters.

Did you know? The temperature of a whale is about the same as yours.

► SKY HIGH

A humpback whale surfaces and blows a column of warm, moist air. As it rises it cools, and the moisture in it condenses into a cloud of tiny water droplets.

▼ DEEP DIVING

Whales feed at different depths. Most dolphins feed close to the surface. The sperm whale holds the diving record. It can descend to about 2,000m/ 6,500ft and stay under water for up to an hour.

Depth		Length of Dive
Surface		common dolphin 15 minutes
		fin whale 20 minutes
610m/ 2000ft		pilot whale 15 minutes
1220m/ 4000ft		
1830m/ 6000ft		
		sperm whale 60 minutes
2440m/ 8000ft		

▼ ONE BLOWHOLE

Like all toothed whales, a bottlenose dolphin has only one blowhole. When the dolphin dives, thick lips of elastic tissue close it to stop water entering, no matter how deep the dive.

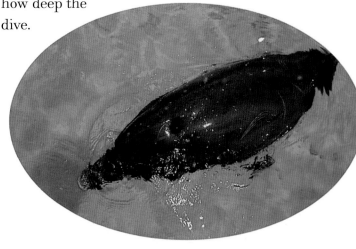

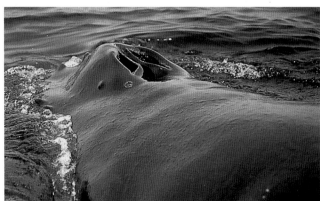

▲ TWO BLOWHOLES

The humpback whale breathes out through a pair of blowholes, located behind a ridge called a splashguard. This helps prevent water from entering the blowholes when the whale is blowing.

13

Whale Brain and Senses

A whale controls its body through its nervous system. The brain is the control point, carrying out functions automatically, but also acting upon information supplied by the senses. The sizes of whale brains vary according to the animal's size. However, dolphins have much bigger brains for their size. Hearing is by far a whale's most important sense. They pick up sounds with tiny ears located just behind the eyes.

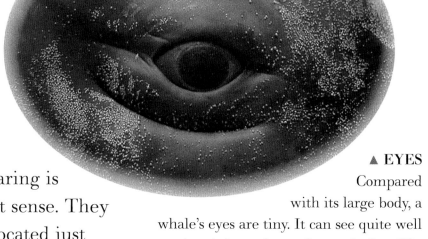

▲ EYES
Compared with its large body, a whale's eyes are tiny. It can see quite well when it is on the surface and often lifts its head out of the water to look around.

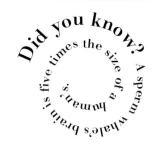

Did you know? A sperm whale's brain is five times the size of a human's.

◄ CLOSE ENCOUNTERS
A group of Atlantic spotted dolphins swim closely together in the seas around the Bahama Islands. Like most other cetaceans, the dolphins often nudge one another and stroke each other with their flippers and tail. Touch plays a very important part in dolphin society, especially in courtship.

◄ SLAP HAPPY

A humpback whale slapping its tail, or lob-tailing, a pastime enjoyed by great whales. Lob-tailing creates a noise like a gunshot in the air, but, more importantly, it will make a loud report underwater. All the other whales in the area will be able to hear the noise.

Cupids and Dolphins
In this Roman mosaic, cupids and dolphins gambol (play) together. In Roman mythology, Cupid was the god of love. Roman artists were inspired by the dolphin's intelligence and gentleness. They saw it as a sacred creature.

◄ BRAINY DOLPHIN?

Some dolphins, such as the bottlenose, have a brain that is much the same size as our own. It is quite a complex brain with many folds.

► IN TRAINING

A bottlenose dolphin swims with its trainer. This species has a particularly large brain for its size. It can be easily trained and has a good memory. It can observe other animals and learn to mimic the way they behave in a short time. It is also good at solving problems, something that we consider a sign of intelligence.

Sounds and Songs

Whales use sounds to communicate with one another, and to find their food. Baleen whales use low-pitched sounds, which have been picked up by underwater microphones as moans, grunts and snores. The toothed whales make higher-pitched sounds, picked up as squeaks, creaks or whistles. Whales also use high-pitched clicks when hunting. They send out beams of sound, which are reflected by objects in their path, such as fish. The whale picks up the reflected sound, or echo, and works out the object's location. This is called echo-location.

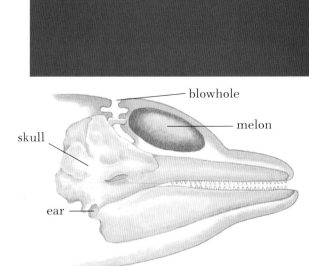

blowhole

melon

skull

ear

◄ ECHO SOUNDINGS
The Amazon river dolphin hunts by echo-location. It sends out up to 80 high-pitched clicks per second. The sound transmits in a beam from a bulge on top of its head. All toothed whales and dolphins hunt in this way.

► SEA CANARIES
A group of belugas, or white whales, swim in a bay in Canada. Belugas' voices can clearly be heard above the surface. This is why they are known as sea canaries. They also produce high-pitched sounds we cannot hear, which they use for echo-location.

▲ MAKING WAVES
A dolphin vibrates the air in its nasal passages to make high-pitched sound waves, which are focused into a beam by the melon – a bulge on its head. The sound beam transmits into the water.

◄ **SUPER SONGSTER**

This male humpback whale is heading for breeding grounds where females are gathering. The male starts singing long and complicated songs. This may be to attract a mate, or to warn other males off its patch. The sound can carry for 30km/18 miles or more.

▼ **LONG SONGS**

This is a voice print of a humpback whale's song, picked up by an underwater microphone. It shows complex musical phrases and melodies. Humpback whales often continue singing for a day or more, repeating the same song.

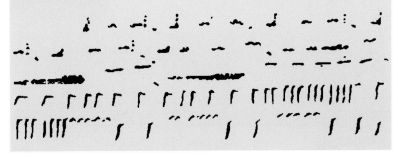

▼

SOUND ECHOES

A sperm whale can locate a giant squid more than 1.6km/1 mile away by transmitting pulses of sound waves into the water and listening. The echo is picked up by the teeth in its lower jaw and the vibrations are sent along the jaw to the ear.

Did you know? A dolphin picks up sounds through its lower jaw.

◄ **ALIEN GREETINGS**

The songs of the humpback whale travel not only through Earth's oceans, but also far out into space. They are among the typical recorded sounds of our world that are being carried by the two Voyager space probes. These probes are now many millions of miles away from earth and are on their way to the stars.

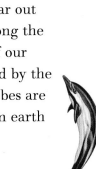

17

Feeding Habits

Most baleen whales feed by taking mouthfuls of seawater containing fish and tiny shrimp-like creatures called krill or plankton, as well as algae, jellyfish, worms and so on. The whale closes its mouth and lifts its tongue, forcing water out through the bristly baleen plates on the upper jaw. The baleen acts like a sieve and holds back the food, which the whale then swallows. Toothed whales feed mainly on fish and squid. They find their prey by echo-location.

▲ CRUNCHY KRILL

These crustaceans, known as krill, form the diet of many baleen whales. Measuring up to 7.6cm/3in long, they swim in vast schools, often covering an area of several square miles. Most krill are found in Antarctic waters.

◀ SCRAPING BY

A grey whale scrapes along the seabed, stirring up sand and ooze. It dislodges tiny crustaceans, called amphipods, and gulps them down. Grey whales feed mostly in summer in the Arctic before they migrate south.

◀ SKIM FEEDING

With its mouth open, a southern right whale filters tiny crustaceans, called copepods, out of the water with its baleen. It eats up to two tons of these plankton daily. It eats so much because of its huge size – up to 80 tons. Usually right whales feed alone, but if food is plentiful, several will feed cruising side by side.

◄ SUCCULENT SQUID

Squid is a food enjoyed by the sperm whale, and it is also eaten by other toothed whales and dolphins. Squid are molluscs, in the same animal phylum as snails and octopuses. Unlike octopuses, they have eight arms and two tentacles, and are called decapods (meaning "ten feet"). Squid swim together in dense schools, many thousand strong. They are fast swimmers.

◄ TOOTHY SMILE

A Ganges river dolphin has more than 100 teeth. The front ones are very long. Ganges river dolphins eat mainly fish, and also take shrimp and crab. They usually feed at night and find their prey by echo-location.

Did you know? A blue whale eats nearly 1,000kg of krill in a single meal.

► LUNCH

Belugas feed on squid and small fish, which are in plentiful supply in the icy ocean. Unlike common dolphins, belugas do not have many teeth. They may simply suck prey into their mouths. Many beaked whales, which also feed on squid, have no teeth suitable for clutching prey.

▲ HUNT THE SQUID

The sperm whale is the largest toothed whale, notable for its huge head and tiny lower jaw. It hunts the giant squid that live in waters around 2,000m/6,500ft deep. At that depth, in total darkness, it hunts its prey by echo-location.

FOCUS ON

1 A killer whale will go hunting by itself if it chances upon a likely victim, such as this lone sea lion. This hungry whale has spotted the sea lion splashing in the surf at the water's edge. With powerful strokes of its tail, it surges towards its intended prey. The whale's tall dorsal fin shows that it is a fully-grown male.

Among the toothed whales, the killer whale, or orca, is the master predator. It feeds on a wider variety of prey than any other whale. It bites and tears its prey to pieces with its fearsome teeth and may also batter them with its powerful tail. It is the only whale to take warm-blooded prey. Fortunately, there is no record of a killer whale ever attacking human beings. As well as fish and squid, a killer whale will hunt seals, penguins, dolphins and porpoises. It may even attack large baleen whales many times its size. Killer whales live in family groups, or pods. They often go hunting together, which greatly improves the chance of success.

2 The sea lion seems totally unaware of what is happening but, in any case, it is nearly helpless in the shallow water. The killer whale is scraping the shore as it homes in for the kill.

Killer Whales

3 Suddenly the killer's head bursts out of the water, and its jaws gape open. Its vicious teeth, curving inwards and backwards, are exposed. It is ready to sink them into its sea lion prey. The killer whale may have fewer teeth than most toothed whales, but they are large and very strong.

4 Now the killer snaps its jaws shut, clamping the sea lion in a vice-like grip. With its prey struggling helplessly, it slides back into deep water to eat its fill. Killer whales sometimes almost beach themselves when they lunge after prey but, helped by the surf, they usually manage to wriggle back into the sea.

The humpback whale usually scoops up water as it lunges forwards and upwards to feed. Grooves in its throat lets the mouth expand to take in tonnes of water containing food, which it filters through its baleen plates. This way of lunge-feeding is typical of the baleen whales known as the rorquals, which also include the blue, fin, sei and minke whales. Before lunge-feeding, humpbacks may blow a circle of bubbles around the fish. The bubbles act like a net to stop the fish escaping.

ON THE LOOKOUT

A humpback whale spy-hops in the feeding grounds of Alaska. It is looking for signs of shoals of fish, such as cod. In the Northern Hemisphere, humpbacks feed mainly on fish. The Southern Hemisphere humpbacks feed mainly on plankton, such as krill.

FORWARD LUNGE

Once in the middle of a shoal, the humpback opens its mouth and lunges forwards. The throat grooves expand as water rushes in. It uses its tongue and cheek muscles to force the water through its baleen plates, leaving the fish behind in its mouth.

Lunging for Lunch

UPWARD LUNGE
Here, the humpback is using a different technique. It sinks below the surface and then flicks its tail to help it to shoot upwards again. With mouth gaping open, it lunges at the fish from below.

RING OF BUBBLES
The surface of the sea is boiling with a ring of frothy bubbles. Unseen, beneath the water, one or more humpback whales swim in circles, letting out air as they do so.

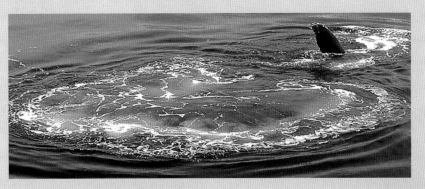

BUBBLE NETTING
The circle of bubbles rises to the surface from the whales circling under the water. It forms a kind of net around a shoal of fish. The whales then swim up to the surface, mouths gaping, to engulf the netted prey.

Swimming

All whales are superb swimmers. All parts of the whale's body help it to move through the water. The driving force comes from the tail fin, or flukes. Using very powerful muscles in the rear third of its body, the whale beats its tail up and down, and the whole body bends. It uses its pectoral fins, or flippers, near the front of the body to steer with. The body itself is streamlined and smooth to help it slip through the water easily. The body can change shape slightly to keep the water flowing smoothly around it. Little ridges under the skin help as well.

▲ STEERING
Among whales, the humpback has by far the longest front flippers. As well as for steering, it uses its flippers for slapping the water. Flipper-slapping seems to be a form of communication.

◀ TAIL POWER
The tail flukes of a grey whale rise into the air before it dives. Whales move their broad tails up and down to drive themselves through the water.

▼ MASSIVE FIN
The dorsal fin of a killer whale projects high into the air. The animal is a swift swimmer, and the fin helps keep its body well balanced. The killer whale has such a large dorsal fin that some experts believe it may help to regulate their body temperature, or even be used in courtship. Most whales and dolphins have a dorsal fin, although some only have a raised hump.

Did you know? A killer whale can swim up to 64kph/40mph.

◀ STREAMLINING

Atlantic spotted dolphins' bodies are beautifully streamlined — shaped so that they slip easily through the water when they move. The dolphin's body is long and rounded, broad in front and becoming narrower toward the tail. Apart from the dorsal fin and flippers, nothing projects from its body. It has no external ears or rear limbs.

▼ HOW A DOLPHIN SWIMS

Dolphins beat their tail flukes up and down by means of the powerful muscles near the tail. The flukes force the water backward at each stroke. As the water is forced back, the dolphin's body is forced forward. Its other fins help guide it through the water. They do not provide propulsion.

◀ SMOOTH SKINNED

This bottlenose dolphin is tailwalking — supporting itself by powerful thrusts of its tail. Unlike most mammals, it has no covering of hair or hair follicles — the dimples in the skin from which the hair grows. Its smooth skin helps the dolphin's body slip through the water.

▼ HOW A FISH SWIMS

It is mainly the tail that provides the power for a fish to swim. The tail has vertical fins, unlike the horizontal fins of the dolphin. It swims by beating its tail and body from side to side.

Focus on

Most whales feed beneath the surface, some often diving deep to reach their food. We can usually identify the species of whale from the way it prepares to dive, or sound. The sperm whale, for example, is one of the species that lifts its tail high into the air before it descends into the ocean. It is the deepest diver of all the whales, sometimes descending to more than a mile in search of squid. It can stay under water for an hour or more before it has to come up for air. As in other whales, its lungs collapse when it dives. It is thought that the great mass of oil in its head helps the whale when diving and surfacing.

1 Two sperm whales swim at the surface. The one on the right is preparing to dive. Its head is in the air, and it fills its lungs with air in a series of blows. The sperm whale's blow projects forward, as in no other whale.

2 The diving whale lashes its tail and accelerates through the water, creating a foaming wake. Now the whale starts the dive, thrusting its bulbous head down and arching its back steeply. The rounded hump on its back rises high into the air. The lumpy knuckles behind the hump become visible as the body arches over.

Diving

3 As the whale's head goes under, the oil in its head freezes and gets heavier on the way down, then melts and becomes lighter again on the way up. If it is going to make a deep dive, the whale may not take another breath for more than an hour.

4 Soon the body disappears with just the tail flukes poking out of the water. The body is now in a vertical position, and that is how it remains as the whale dives swiftly into the deep. Descending at speeds of more than 150m/500ft per minute, it is soon in darkness, scanning its surroundings by beams of sound for the squid on which it feeds.

Social Life

Every day we meet, work, play and communicate with other people. We are sociable animals. Some whales are also sociable and live together. Sperm whales live in groups of up to about 50. A group may be a breeding school of females and young or a bachelor school of young males. Older male sperm whales live alone, except in the breeding season. Beluga whales often live in groups of several hundred. Baleen whales are not as sociable. They move singly or in small groups, probably because of their huge appetite – they could not find enough food if they lived close together.

▲ HERD INSTINCT

Beluga whales gather together in very large groups, or herds, and they mostly stay in these herds for life. Many of the animals in this group, pictured in the Canadian Arctic, have calves. These can be recognized, not only by their smaller size, but also because of their darker skin.

Did you know? Dolphins will nudge a sick member of the group up to the surface, so it does not drown.

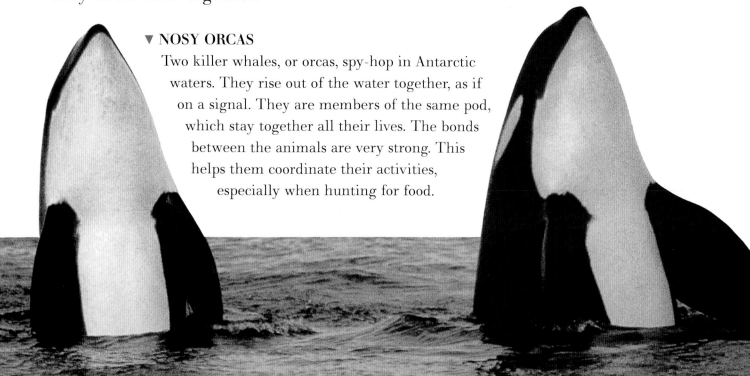

▼ NOSY ORCAS

Two killer whales, or orcas, spy-hop in Antarctic waters. They rise out of the water together, as if on a signal. They are members of the same pod, which stay together all their lives. The bonds between the animals are very strong. This helps them coordinate their activities, especially when hunting for food.

◄ STAYING CLOSE

Two Atlantic spotted dolphins swim with their young. The young's spots will not start to appear until the animals are about a year old. As with many other species, the young stay very close to their parents most of the time.

▼ HUMAN CONTACT

A bottlenose dolphin swims alongside a boy. These dolphins live in social groups but lone outcasts, or animals that have become separated from their group, often approach humans.

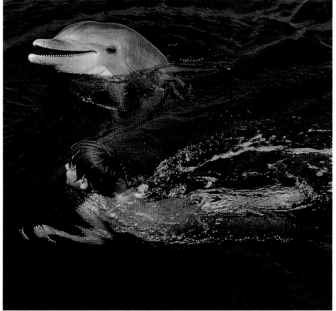

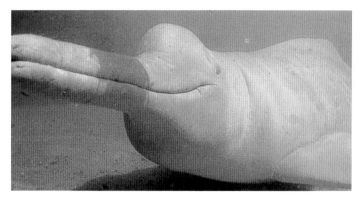

▲ SOLITARY SWIMMER

An Amazon river dolphin rests on the river bed. It spends most of its life alone, or with just one other. This solitary existence is typical of river dolphins, but untypical of most ocean dolphins and whales.

► PILOT ERROR

These long-finned pilot whales are stranded on a beach. Pilot whales usually live in large groups, with strong bonds between group members. One whale may strand itself on a beach. The others may try to help it and get stranded themselves.

The Mating Game

Whales mate at certain times of year. Baleen whales mate during the late autumn after the whales have migrated to their warm-water breeding grounds. One whale will mate a number of times with different partners. Several males may attempt to steer a female into a mating position. Often the males fight each other for the chance to mate. Male narwhals even fence with their long tusks. But mating rituals can also be gentle, with the males and females caressing one another with their flippers.

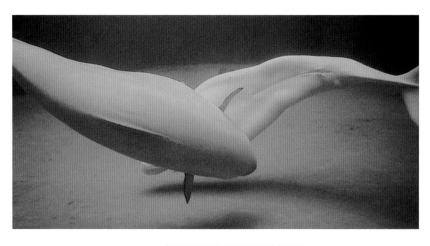

▲ WHITE WEDDING
A pair of belugas show interest in each other. Males and females spend the year in separate groups, only mixing in the mating season. They mate and calve in bays in the far north.

◀ LOVE SONG
Whales attract mates by body language and sound. This humpback can pinpoint another's position, and perhaps exchange messages, over great distances.

◀ MATING TIFFS
Two grey whales court in the winter breeding grounds off Baja California, Mexico. Usually, a group of males fights for the right to mate with a female, causing commotion in the water. The female might mate many times with them.

◀ ROLLOVER
Courtship for these southern right whales is nearly over. The male *(top)* has succeeded in getting the female to roll over on her back and is moving into the mating position.

The Fabulous Unicorn

In the breeding season, male narwhals fight each other using their long tusks, which often break. Long ago, when these small whales were little known, people found the tusks and wondered what kind of creature they came from. This may have led to the idea of the unicorn, a horse-like beast with a long spiral horn (like the narwhal's) on its forehead.

▼ BIG BABY
A sperm whale calf snuggles up to its mother. A calf might measure up to 4.5m/15ft long when born, nearly 15 months after mating took place. The mother feeds it for a year or more, leaving it only to dive deep for food.

◀ BELLY TO BELLY
A pair of southern right whales mate, belly to belly. The male has inserted his long penis into the female to inject his sperm. Usually, the male's penis stays hidden in the body behind a genital slit. It will be nine months or more before the female gives birth to a single calf.

Did you know? Female sperm whales can mate at the age of 8. Males cannot mate until they are nearly 20.

31

Focus on

BIRTHDAY
A bottlenose dolphin gives birth. The baby is born tail-first. This birth is taking place near the bottom of an aquarium. In the wild, birth takes place close to the surface so the baby can surface quickly and start breathing.

After mating, the female whale becomes pregnant and a baby whale starts to grow inside her body. After about a year, the calf is ready to be born. By now it can weigh, in the case of the blue whale, up to 2.5 tons. The first thing the calf must do is take a breath, and the mother or another whale may help it to the surface. Soon it finds one of the mother's nipples to suck the rich milk in her mammary glands (breasts). It suckles for several months until it learns to take solid food such as fish. Mother and calf may spend most of the time alone, or join nursery schools with other mothers and calves.

SUCKLING
A beluga mother suckles her young under water. Her fatty milk is very nutritious, and the calf grows rapidly. It will drink milk for up to two years. At birth the calf's body is dark grey, but it slowly lightens as the calf matures.

Bringing Up Baby

AT PLAY

A young Atlantic spotted dolphin and its mother play together, twisting, turning, rolling and touching each other with their flippers. During play, the young dolphin learns the skills it will need later in life when it has to fend for itself. The youngster is darker than its mother and has no spots. These do not start to appear until it is about a year old.

TOGETHERNESS

A humpback whale calf sticks closely to its mother as she swims slowly in Hawaiian waters. The slipstream, or water flow, created by the mother's motion helps pull it along. For the first few months of its life, it will not stray far from its mother's side.

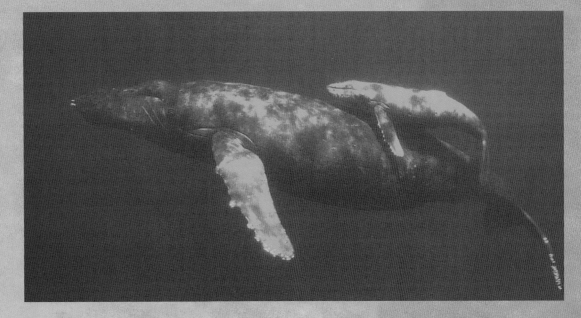

Having Fun

Dolphins have long delighted people with their acrobatic antics. They somersault, ride the bow waves of boats and go surfing. Dusky and spinner dolphins are particularly lively. Some antics have a purpose, such as sending signals to other dolphins. But often the animals seem to perform just for fun. In most animal species only the young play. In whale and dolphin society, adults play too. Southern right whales play a sailing game. They hang in the water with their heads down and tails in the air. The tails act like sails and catch the wind, and they are blown along.

▲ PLAYFUL PAIR

Two Atlantic spotted dolphins jostle as they play with a sea fan. Dolphins spend much of their time playing, especially the younger ones. They make up games, using anything they can find. Their games can last for hours.

▼ JUMPING FOR JOY

A pair of bottlenose dolphins leaps high, leaving the water together, as if they have rehearsed their act. They seem to jump for joy, but their activity may have a social function within their family group.

▶ PORPOISING ON PURPOSE

A group of long-snouted spinner dolphins go porpoising, taking long, low leaps as they swim. They churn the water behind them into a foam. Many dolphins do this, in order to travel fast on the water's surface.

Did you know? Killer whales like brushing against each other as they swim at high speed.

◀ RIDING THE WAKE

A Pacific white-sided dolphin surfs the waves. This is one of the most acrobatic of the dolphins. It is often seen bow-riding in front of boats. Other species of dolphin also like to ride in the waves left in the wake of passing boats.

Did you know? The rough skin on a porpoise's back may be for giving calves piggy-back rides.

▶ AQUATIC ACROBAT

This dusky dolphin is throwing itself high into the air. It twists and turns, spins and performs somersaults. This display is like a roll call – to check that every dolphin in the group is present and ready to go hunting. It is repeated after hunting, to gather the group together once more.

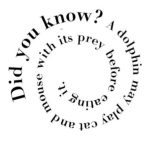

Did you know? A dolphin may play cat and mouse with its prey before eating it.

Focus on

A whale leaps from the sea and crashes back to the surface in a shower of spray. This activity, called breaching, is common among humpbacks. Some may breach up to 200 times in succession. When one animal starts breaching, others follow suit. Whales put on other displays as well, including slapping their flippers and tail on the surface. These activities could, like breaching, be some form of signalling. Spy-hopping is another activity, often done to look for signs of fish to eat.

BREACHING

Propelled by powerful thrusts of its tail, the humpback launches its vast bulk into the air, twisting as it does so. For a creature weighing up to 30 tons, this is no mean feat. As breaching ends, it crashes back to the surface with a splash. This time it lands on its back, with one of its flippers up in the air.

FLIPPER-FLOPPING

The humpback swims on the surface, raising one flipper in the air. It rolls over and slaps the flipper on the water several times, perhaps to warn off rivals. Its flipper-flopping is noisy because its flippers are so large.

Whales on Display

WHAT A FLUKE!

The humpback raises its tail in the air during the display known as lob-tailing or tail-slapping. The tail is also exposed when the whale is about to dive, an action called fluking. It is easy to tell if a humpback is lob-tailing or fluking. In fluking, the tail disappears below the surface quietly.

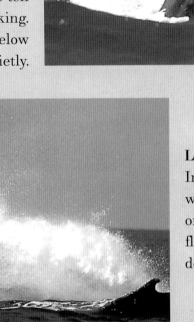

LOB-TAILING

In lob-tailing, the tail slaps on the water with a noise like a gunshot. The only other time a humpback shows its flukes is when it is about to go on a deep dive.

SPY-HOPPING

The humpback on the right of the picture is spy-hopping. It positions itself vertically in the water and pokes out its head until its eyes are showing. Then it has a good look round. The other humpback here is doing the opposite, poking out its tail, ready to lob-tail.

Where Whales are Found

Whales are found in all the world's oceans. Some kinds live all over, while others are found only in a certain area. They may stay in the same place all year long, or migrate from one area to another with the seasons. Some whales stick to shallow coastal areas, others prefer deep waters. Some live in the cool northern or southern parts of the world. Others are more at home in tropical regions near the Equator. Some species even live in rivers.

▼ **OCEAN WANDERER**
A humpback whale surfaces to blow while swimming at Cape Cod off the north-east coast of North America. In winter, the humpback feeds in high latitudes. It migrates to low latitudes to breed during the summer.

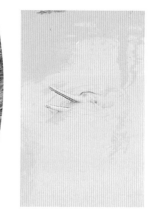

▲ **MUDDY WATERS**
The mud-laden waters of the River Amazon in South America are the habitat of the Amazon river dolphin. Here, one shows off its teeth. This species ranges along the Amazon and its tributaries.

Did you know? Some dolphins come and go between salt water and fresh water.

◄ **WORLDWIDE WHALE**
Among ice-floes in the Arctic Ocean, a killer whale, or orca, hunts for prey. Orcas are found in all the oceans. They live in coastal areas but may venture out to the open ocean. They also swim in the surf along the shore, and may beach to snatch their prey.

▶ **SNOW WHITE**
These belugas, or white whales, are in Hudson Bay, Canada. These cold-water animals live around coasts in the far north of North America, Europe and Asia. They venture into estuaries and even up rivers. In winter they hunt in the pack ice in the Arctic.

◀ **TROPICAL MELONS**
A pod of melon-headed whales is shown swimming in the Pacific Ocean. These creatures prefer warm waters and are found in subtropical and tropical regions in both the Northern and Southern Hemispheres. They generally stay in deep water, keeping well away from land.

▶ **WIDE RANGER**
A bottlenose dolphin lunges through the surf in the sunny Bahamas. This animal is one of the most wide-ranging of the dolphins, being found in temperate to tropical waters in both the Northern and Southern Hemispheres. It is also found in enclosed seas such as the Mediterranean and the Red Sea. Mostly it stays in coastal waters. When bottlenose dolphins migrate to warmer areas, they lose weight. When they return to colder climes, their blubber increases again.

Migration

Grey whales spend the summer months feeding in the Arctic Ocean. Many of the females are pregnant. Before winter comes, the whales head south toward Mexico for warmer waters, where the females give birth to their calves, which stand a better chance of surviving in the warmer waters. Mating occurs in late winter. In the spring, the greys head north to the Arctic. Their annual journey between feeding and breeding grounds involves a round trip of some 20,000km/12,400 miles. The humpbacks also take part in long migrations. Most of the other large rorquals and the right whales seem to undergo similar migrations.

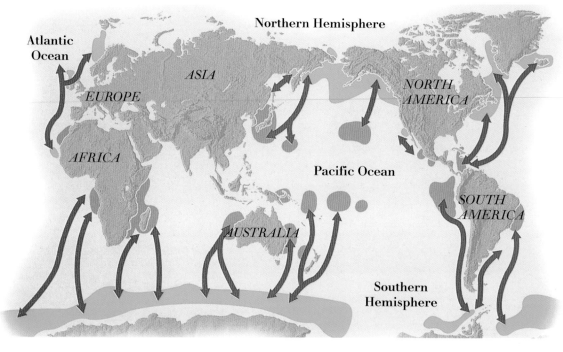

Migration
This map shows the routes taken by humpback whales during their annual migrations between their summer feeding and winter breeding grounds. There are at least three main groups, two in the Northern and one in the Southern Hemisphere.

KEY TO MAP

 breeding grounds
 feeding grounds

◄ SUMMER FEEDING
Two Southern Hemisphere humpbacks feed in the Antarctic Ocean during the summer months. This is when the krill and other plankton they feed on thrive. The whales have taken huge mouthfuls of water, which they sieve for plankton using the baleen on their upper jaws.

▼ RIGHT LOCATION

The tail fluke of a southern right
whale is thrust into the air as the
whale sails. This whale is one of
a group of right whales in winter
breeding grounds off the coast of
Argentina. By summer
the whales will have
returned south to feed
in the Antarctic
Ocean.

Did you know? Grey whales make longer migrations than any other mammal.

▲ WINTER BREEDING

It is early winter and two humpbacks have
migrated north from the Antarctic to a
shallow bay on the coast of eastern
Australia. A large group of humpbacks
will mate here and, about 12 months later,
the females will give birth.

▼ MATING GREYS

In the winter breeding grounds of
Baja California, a grey whale
surfaces. They spend about three
months in the region, where
mating and (two years
later) births take
place.

High and Dry

Dead whales are often found washed up, or stranded, on the seashore. Live whales are sometimes found too, particularly open ocean species, such as sperm whales. Some live whales probably strand when they become ill. Others strand when they lose their sense of direction. Whales are thought to find their way using the Earth's magnetism as a kind of map. Any change in the magnetism may cause them to turn the wrong way and head for the shore. Mass strandings also take place, with scores of whales left helpless. This happens particularly among sociable species, such as the pilot whales.

Did you know? When people help stranded whales, the whales often swim back and get stranded again.

▲ BEACHED DOLPHIN
This Atlantic white-sided dolphin is stranded on a beach in the Orkney Islands. The dolphins usually travel in big groups, so mass strandings occur too.

▲ WAITING FOR THE TIDE
People come to the aid of stranded long-finned pilot whales in New Zealand. They cover the whales to prevent sunburn and throw water over them to keep their skin moist.

◄ RARE STRANDING

Marine biologists examine a stranded Stejneger's beaked whale. Beaked whales are among the least known of all the cetaceans. Most of our knowledge about them comes from occasional strandings. Several beaked whales, such as this one, have a large tooth protruding from the jaws.

Did you know? Whales stranded in Britain belong to the monarch.

► IN THE SHALLOWS

Three belugas became stranded in shallow water as the tide went out. Polar bears may attack when they are beached. Belugas rarely become stranded, and usually survive until the tide comes in again.

▼ BIG FIN

A huge fin whale has become beached on a mudflat. This animal is dead, but even if it were alive, it would be impossible to return to the water. When a whale of this size is not supported by water its internal organs collapse. Scientists examine stranded bodies to learn about whales.

Grey and Right Whales

Grey whales and the three species of right whale, including the bowhead, are all filter-feeders with baleen plates in their upper jaws. The bowhead has the longest baleen of all, while the grey whale has short baleen. Unlike most baleen whales, the grey whale feeds mainly on the seabed. It is found only in the Northern Hemisphere, but there are right whales in both hemispheres. Right whales were named by whalers because they were the right whales to catch for their high yields of oil and baleen. They swam slowly, they could be approached easily and floated when dead.

▲ **MOTTLED MAMMAL**
The long, narrow head of a grey whale breaks the surface. Its closed blowholes are in the middle of the picture. The head is covered here and there with clusters of barnacles and lice. This, together with lighter body patches, gives the animal a mottled appearance.

◀ **LIVELY LOB**
Near the coast of Argentina in South America, a southern right whale is lob-tailing. In seconds, its tail will crash down on the surface with a smack that will echo off the cliffs on the shore. The noise will be heard by other whales, many kilometres/ miles away. Right whales often lob-tail and also do headstands, waving their tails in the air.

▲ **WHITE CHIN**
A bowhead whale thrusts its head out of the water, exposing its unique white chin, covered with black patches. The skin is smooth, with no growths like those on the skin of the northern and southern right whales.

Did you know? We know a lot about grey whales because they stay in shallow waters near the coast.

◄ BEARDED

A southern right whale cruises in the South Atlantic. One distinctive feature of this whale is the deeply curved jawline. Another is its beard and bonnet. These are large growths on the whale's chin and nose, which become infested with barnacles.

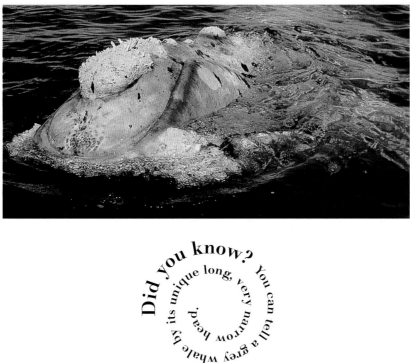

◄ HAIRY MONSTER

The northern right whale lives in the North Atlantic. Whalers used to call the crusty hard skin on its head a bonnet or rock garden. Lice and barnacles live on this skin, which can grow enormous. Right whales are the hairiest of all whales, keeping more hair after birth than other cetaceans. It even grows facial hair!

Did you know? You can tell a grey whale by its unique long, very narrow head.

► BRISTLY JAWS

A grey whale opens its mouth, showing the baleen plates on its upper jaw. The baleen is quite short, stiff and coarse. The whale uses it to filter out the tiny creatures it digs out of the seabed when feeding. Grey whales are not shy and sometimes swim up to the boats of whale-watchers.

Rorquals

The rorquals are a family of baleen whales that includes the largest creature ever to live, the blue whale. They are named after the grooves on their throat – the word rorqual means a furrow. All rorquals, except the humpback, have a long streamlined body with a sharp nose and a dorsal fin set well back. They can swim at up to 30kph/20mph. The humpback is a slower swimmer with a chunkier body. It has knobbly flippers and a hump in front of the dorsal fin. It is famous for the songs it sings. The minke whale is the smallest rorqual. Bryde's whale lives mainly in tropical and subtropical waters, while the other rorquals often venture into colder waters as well, often venturing into polar waters in the summer.

▼ **TINY MINKE**

The minke whale grows to only about one-third of the size of the blue whale and never exceeds 10 tons in weight. It has a slim snout and a curved dorsal fin. Its flippers are short and can be marked with a broad white band.

▲ **WHALE WITH A HUMP**

This picture of a humpback whale shows the feature that gives it its name very well. Its small dorsal fin sits on top of a pronounced hump on its back. This profile view of the animal also shows the prominent splash guard on its head in front of the blowholes.

Did you know? Humpback whales can live to age 95.

▼ **KNOBBLY FLIPPER**

A humpback whale swims on the surface, with one of its flippers up in the air like a boat sail. The flippers of the humpback are by far the most distinctive of all the whales. They are sturdy and very long – up to a third of the length of the whale's body. The flippers have knobs along their front edge.

flipper

◄ BIG GULP
A blue whale feeds in Californian waters. It has taken in a mouthful of water containing thousands of the tiny shrimp-like krill it feeds on. The grooves on its throat that allow its mouth to expand can be clearly seen. A blue whale typically has between 60 and 90 of these grooves.

► DRIPPING FLUKES
A blue whale fluking, with its tail flukes rising out of the water before the animal dives. Among rorquals, only blue and humpback whales expose their flukes before diving. The humpback's tail flukes are quite different. They are knobbly at the rear edges and have white markings on the underside.

Did you know? A blue whale's heart is about the size of a small car.

◄ SEI WHALE
The sei whale can be found in most of the oceans. It feeds in the cool Arctic or Antarctic waters during the summer and migrates to warmer waters in the winter to breed. With a length of up to about 18m/60ft, it is slightly larger than the similar looking Bryde's whale.

47

Sperm and White Whales

The sperm and the white whales are two families of toothed whales. The sperm whale and dwarf and pygmy sperm whales have an organ in their head called the spermaceti organ, which is filled with wax. The wax may help the animals when they dive and may play a part in focusing the sound waves they use for echolocation. The sperm whale and the two white whales (the beluga and the narwhal) have no dorsal fin. The sperm whale has teeth only on its lower jaw. The beluga has up to 20 teeth in each of its jaws, but the narwhal has only two. In the male narwhal, one of the teeth grows into a spiral tusk, measuring up to 3m/10ft long.

◄ BABY EYES

The eye of a sperm whale calf. Like all whales, the sperm whale has tiny eyes compared with those of most other mammals. But this does not matter because when the whale dives to feed, it descends deep into the ocean where light never reaches. It depends on its superb echolocation system to find its prey.

Did you know? Perfume is made from foul-smelling wax made in sperm whales' guts.

◄ LOOKING AROUND

A beluga raises its head above the water to look around – they are inquisitive creatures. Belugas have quite a short head with a rounded melon. Unusually for whales, it has a noticeable neck, allowing it to turn its head. It also has a wide range of facial expressions and often appears to be smiling.

Did you know? A sperm whale can dive as deep as 3,000m/10,000ft in search of squid.

◄ COW AND CALF
A sperm whale cow swims with her calf. Cows suckle their young for at least two years in a nursery group with other cows and calves. This picture shows the sperm whale's unique body shape, with its huge blunt snout. The sperm whale does not have a dorsal fin, just a triangular lump on its back.

► HIGH SOCIETY
This pod of belugas is swimming in Arctic waters off the coast of Canada. Belugas are usually found in such pods because they are very social animals. Note the typical body characteristics, including broad stubby flippers and the lack of a dorsal fin.

▼ LONG IN THE TOOTH
In freezing Arctic waters a male narwhal comes to the surface to blow, its long tusk raised. The tusk has a spiral shape and can be up to 3m/10ft long. It is one of the narwhal's two teeth. A small number of male narwhals have twin tusks.

tusk

▲ BULKY LIKE A BELUGA
The narwhal's stocky body is much like that of the beluga. Both grow up to about 5m/16ft long and weigh up to 1,500kg/3,300lb. The main difference is that while the beluga is white, the narwhal is mostly a mottled dark and light grey.

Beaked, Pilot and Killer Whales

Beaked whales are named after their beak, which is rather like that of many kinds of dolphin. Unlike dolphins, they have hardly any teeth — most have just two. Beaked whales live mainly in the deep ocean, and little is known about them. Pilot and killer whales, or orcas, are better known. They are part of the dolphin family and, like many dolphins, tend to live in quite large groups. Because pilot whales and orcas are mostly black, they are often called blackfish. The orca is the largest and best known of the family and is a fierce predator.

▲ A TELLING TAIL
A killer whale lob-tails. Its tail is black on top but mainly white underneath, with a distinct notch in the middle. Note also the pointed tips of the flukes.

◀ KILLER LEAP
A killer whale, or orca, leaps high into the air while breaching in Alaskan waters. The whale may twist and turn before it falls back to the surface with a resounding splash. Look at this killer whale's broad paddle-shaped flippers. The size and shape of the flippers and the dorsal fin mark this specimen as a male.

Did you know? Killer whales have never been known to attack humans in the wild.

◄ CRUISING PILOT

The short-finned pilot whale has a broad, bulbous head, and is for this reason sometimes called the pothead whale. It has sickle-shaped flippers and a curved dorsal fin. This pilot whale prefers tropical and subtropical regions. The long-finned pilot whale is similar, but with slightly longer flippers, and lives in the Southern Hemisphere in both cool and warm waters.

► WHITE LIPS

A pod of melon-headed whales swim close together. One of them is spy-hopping, and shows its melon-shaped head. Note its white lips.

◄ SLEEK LINES

Note the streamlined body of the killer whale as it comes out of the water while performing at Sea World in California. The picture shows its white patches behind the eye and at the side, and the white chin. There is a greyish saddle patch behind the dorsal fin.

▼ FALSE TEETH

A false killer whale spy-hops. False killer whales have as many as 20 teeth in each jaw. It does not look much like the killer whale and is much smaller. It has no white patches and its head is more slender.

► LONER

A beaked whale swims alone. Most spend a lot of time alone or with one or two others. They prefer deep waters, and some species dive very deep indeed.

Oceanic Dolphins

Dolphins are the most common of all cetaceans. They are swift swimmers and have sleek, streamlined bodies with, usually, a prominent dorsal fin. They have dark grey backs and white or pale grey bellies. Many dolphins have contrasting stripes along the sides. About half the dolphin species have a long beak, and as many as 250 teeth. The rest have short beaks and fewer teeth. Dolphins can be found in most oceans, but not usually in the cold waters of far northern or far southern regions. Most are highly sociable, some swimming together in groups of hundreds.

◄ STRIKING STRIPES

Distinctive black and white striped bodies tell us that these two animals are southern right whale-dolphins. The back is jet black, while the beak, forehead, belly and flippers are white.

▼ PORPOISING DOLPHINS

A group of common dolphins is porpoising – taking long, low leaps. They have a long beak and yellow markings on their sides. The dark skin on the upper back looks rather like a saddle. This is why it is also called the saddleback dolphin.

Did you know? Dolphins make loud noises when hunting to panic fish into bunching together.

◄ **GREAT LEAPERS**

Two bottlenose dolphins launch themselves with great energy several metres/feet into the air. Their bodies are mainly grey. The head of the bottlenose dolphin is more rounded than that of most other beaked dolphins.

► **BLUNT HEADS**

A group of Risso's dolphins is easy to recognize by their blunt heads and tall dorsal fins. Their bodies are mainly grey on the back and sides. The skin becomes paler with age, and some old adults are almost all white.

▼ **PALE FACE**

The odd-looking Irrawaddy dolphin has a rounded head and a distinct neck, rather like the beluga. Its flippers are large and curved. It is found in rivers and estuaries, and also coastal waters from south of India as far as northern Australia.

Dolphin Rescue

An old Greek tale tells of a famed poet and musician named Arion. After a concert tour, sailors on the ship that was taking him home set out to kill him for his money. They granted his request to sing a final song. Then he jumped overboard. He did not drown because a dolphin, attracted by his beautiful song, carried him to the shore.

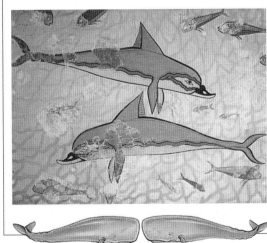

Porpoises and River Dolphins

Porpoises look rather like dolphins, yet they form a separate cetacean family. They are smaller than most dolphins and do not have a typical dolphin beak. Their teeth are different, being spade-like instead of cone-shaped. Most porpoises are shy. The rare river dolphins form a separate family. They have a long slender beak and a rounded forehead. Their flexible neck allows their head to turn, unlike oceanic dolphins. In the muddy waters where they mostly live, they use echo-location rather than their poor eyesight to find the fish and other creatures they feed on.

▲ BEAKED BOTO

The Amazon river dolphin, or boto, has the typical long beak of the river dolphins. Its skin tone varies from pale bluish-grey to pink. It has no dorsal fin, just a fleshy ridge on its back.

◀ RESTING PORPOISE

A Dall's porpoise displays the body features of its species. It has a stocky black body, with a large white patch on the sides and belly. Its dorsal fin and tail flukes have flashes of white as well. Unlike most porpoises, which are shy, the Dall's porpoise loves to bow-ride fast boats.

▼ RARE SNEEZER

Like all river dolphins, the Yangtze river dolphin, or baiji, has poor sight. Its blowhole is circular and its blow sounds like a sneeze! Considered the most endangered cetacean in the world, this dolphin may now be extinct.

Did you know? The harbour porpoise is rarely seen in harbours.

▶ FAST AND FURIOUS

Dall's porpoises are the most energetic of all the porpoises. Their swimming is fast and furious. They kick up great fountains of spray as they thrust themselves through the surface of the water.

▶ NOISY SNORTER

The harbour porpoise seldom comes near boats. It has a noisy, snorting blow. Its general appearance is dark grey on the back with paler patches on the flanks. Its belly is white, and it has black flippers and lips.

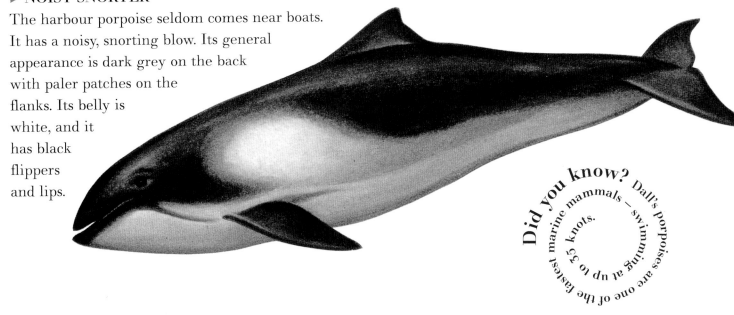

Did you know? Dall's porpoises are one of the fastest marine mammals – swimming at up to 35 knots.

◀ DOLPHIN OR PORPOISE?

Porpoises are close relatives of dolphins, but they belong to a different family with different body features. Scientists can take advantage of strandings such as this one to study these very shy creatures.

55

Similar Swimmers

Whales are not the only aquatic mammals. Other examples include otters and seals. Seals are well adapted to life in the water, with a sleek, streamlined body and flippers. They have some fur, but it is the thick layer of fatty blubber under the skin that keeps them warm in the water. It also insulates against the cold air when seals are on land. The dugong and the manatee are also at home in the water. Often called sea cows, these creatures have a bulky seal-like body. They live in rivers and coastal waters in tropical and subtropical regions.

▲ BEAR AT SEA

The polar bear drifts on pack ice in the Arctic Ocean, often taking to the water to hunt seals. In addition to a thick layer of blubber, a polar bear has a thick furry coat to protect it from the Arctic climate.

◄ FIN-FOOTED

The Californian sea lion swims using powerful strokes of its front flippers. Its body is much more adapted to the water than an otter's, with its paddle-like flippers. Its body is partly hairy, partly smooth.

Did you know? Whales were probably descended from a four-legged land mammal called a mesonychid.

► FURRY SWIMMER

The otter is at home on land or in water. Its four-legged, furry body is adapted for life in the water. Its legs are short, and its toes are webbed, making efficient paddles. Its fur is waterproof.

▲ WHALE-LIKE

The whale shark is not a whale, but the biggest fish of all – a harmless member of the shark family. The whale shark is more than 15m/50ft long. It feeds on plankton, which it takes in through its gaping mouth. It sieves out the plankton from the water through a special gill structure.

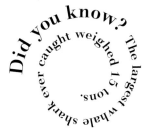

Did you know? The largest whale shark ever caught weighed 15 tons.

◀ SEA COW

A dugong swims in the Pacific Ocean, just off Australia. Unlike the seals, which leave the water to breed on land, dugongs spend all their time in the sea. They have no hind limbs, but a tail, similar to that of a whale. The alternative name for the creature – sea cow – is a good one because the animal feeds on sea grasses.

▶ EXCAVATOR

The walrus is a mammal of the seal family. Like the true seals, it has no external ears and it swims by means of its rear flippers. It feeds mainly on the seabed, using its whiskers to locate buried clams and its tough snout to grub them out. It excavates clams by squirting a high pressure jet of water from its mouth into the clam's burrow.

Whale Slaughter

The baleen whales and sperm whale are so big that they have no natural predators. Until a few hundred years ago, the oceans teemed with them. In the 15th and 16th centuries, whaling grew into a huge industry. Whales were killed for blubber, which could be rendered down into oils for candles and lamps. The industry expanded following the invention of an explosive harpoon gun in the 1860s, and by the 1930s nearly 50,000 whales a year were taken in Antarctica. In 1988, commercial whaling was banned.

▲ WHALE SOAP
The sperm whale was once a prime target for whalers. They were after the waxy spermaceti from the organ in the whale's forehead. This was used to make soap.

► DEADLY STRUGGLE
Whalers row out from a big ship to harpoon a whale in the early 1800s. It was a dangerous occupation in those days because the dying whales could easily smash the small boats to pieces.

Did you know? Whale blubber was made into lipstick and other sorts of make-up.

▼ FIN WHALING
A modern whaler finishes cutting up a fin whale. A few whales are still caught legally for scientific purposes, but their meat ends up on the table in some countries. The fin whale used to be a major target for whalers because of its size.

◀ PILOT MASSACRE
Every year in the Faroe Islands of the North Atlantic pods of pilot whales are killed, a traditional practice that has not been stopped. The blood of the dying whales turns the sea red.

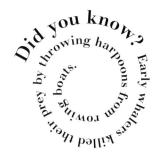

Did you know? Early whalers killed their prey by throwing harpoons from rowing boats.

▶ KILLER NET
This striped dolphin died when it was caught in a drift net. It became entangled and was unable to rise to the surface to breathe. Tens of thousands of dolphins drown each year because of nets cast into the oceans.

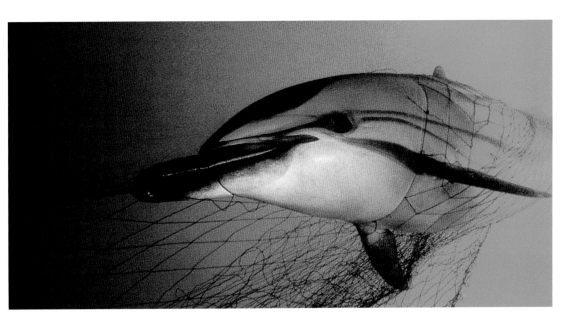

Did you know? In the 1800s baleen was used to make umbrellas.

'Whale Tale'
Moby Dick *was written in 1851 by Herman Melville. The one-legged Captain Ahab searches for a great white whale (a sperm whale) called Moby Dick. Eventually he harpoons Moby Dick, but he and all but one of his crew die.*

THE SPERMACETI WHALE

Whale Conservation

If full-scale whaling had continued, many of the great whales would now be extinct. Even today, only a few thousand blue whales, right whales and bowhead whales remain. Because they are slow breeders, it will take a long time for numbers to recover. However the grey whale and the humpback whale appear to be recovering well. These two whales are very popular among whale-watchers because they are so approachable. Whale-watching has made people aware of what remarkable creatures whales are and why they must be protected.

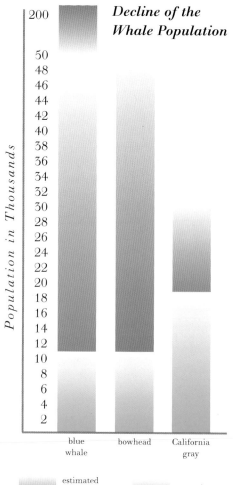

Decline of the Whale Population

Population in Thousands

200
50
48
46
44
42
40
38
36
34
32
30
28
26
24
22
20
18
16
14
12
10
8
6
4
2

blue whale | bowhead | California gray

estimated original population

present population

Did you know? The first whale sanctuary was set up in 1945.

▲ GREY GREETING

A grey whale surfaces near a boat off the Pacific coast of Mexico. It is winter, and the greys have migrated to these warmer breeding grounds from the far north. Because these animals stay close to the shore, they are easy to reach by boat.

▲ WHALE RECOVERY

By the middle of the 20th century, the blue, bowhead and grey whales were close to extinction. Then whaling was banned. Now populations are recovering.

▼ HUMPBACK SPECTACULAR

A humpback whale breaches. It hurls its 30-ton bulk into the air, belly up, and will soon crash back to the surface. Out of all the activities that whale-watchers come to see, this one is by far the most spectacular.

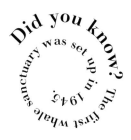

▶ FRIENDLY FLIPPER

One bottlenose dolphin character, called Flipper (played by several dolphins), starred in a series of TV shows and films. These focused attention on how intelligent dolphins are, yet how vulnerable they are, too.

Did you know? You can adopt your own whale by contacting your own local whale and dolphin society.

◀ WHALE-WATCHING

A boatload of whale-watchers sees the tail flukes of a humpback whale disappear as the animal starts to dive. The boat is cruising off the New England coast of the United States where some populations of humpbacks feed during the summer months.

Did you know? Some countries continue to hunt whales.

▶ ENTERTAINING ORCA

A killer whale, or orca, leaps high out of the water at a dolphinarium, drawing applause from the huge crowd watching. In the wild, the killer whale is a deadly predator, but in captivity – with all its meals provided – it is docile and friendly. However, the benefits of keeping these creatures in captivity are not certain.

GLOSSARY

A

Antarctic
The icy region around the South Pole and the Southern Ocean, including the continent of Antarctica.

Arctic
The region around the North Pole.

B

baleen
A tough and flexible material, which forms comb-like plates in the upper jaw of baleen whales.

baleen whale
A whale that has baleen plates in its mouth instead of teeth.

beak
The protruding jaws of a whale or dolphin.

blow
The cloud of moist air that is blown from a whale's blowhole when it breathes out.

blowhole
The nostril of a whale. Baleen whales have two blowholes, toothed whales have one.

blubber
The layer of fatty tissue beneath the skin of a whale that acts as insulation against cold water.

bow-riding
Swimming on the bow wave in front of a moving boat.

breaching
Leaping out of the water and falling back with a great splash.

bull
A male whale.

C

calf
A baby whale.

cetacean
A whale, dolphin or porpoise, all of which belong to the animal order Cetacea.

cow
A female whale.

crustacean
A creature with a hard body that lives in the sea. Shrimp and krill are crustaceans.

D

dolphin
A small, toothed whale that has cone-shaped teeth.

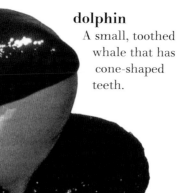

dorsal fin
The usually triangular fin on the back of a whale's body.

E

echo-location
The method toothed whales use to find their prey. They send out pulses of high-pitched sounds and listen for the echoes produced when the pulses are reflected by objects in their path.

extinction
When a species of living thing dies out.

F

flipper
A whale's paddle-like forelimbs.

flukes
The tail of a whale.

fluking
Raising the fluke (tail) into the air before diving.

K

krill
Tiny crustaceans that are the main food for many of the baleen whales.

L

lob-tailing
The action of raising the tail into the air and then slapping it down on the surface of the water.

M

mammal
An animal that has warm blood and breathes air. Female mammals feed their offspring on milk from their mammary glands.

mating
When a male and female unite to reproduce.

melon
The rounded forehead of a toothed whale. It is thought to help direct the sounds the animal uses for echo-location.

migration
The regular journey taken by some animals from one part of the world to another and back at different times of the year.

P

pectoral fin
An alternative name for flipper.

plankton
Tiny sea creatures and plants. They form the basic foodstuff for all life in the oceans.

pod
A group of whales.

polar region
The area around the North or South Pole, where it is very cold.

porpoise
A small toothed whale with spade-shaped teeth.

porpoising
Leaping in and out of the water while swimming fast.

predator
An animal that hunts other animals (prey) for its food.

pregnant
When a female animal has a baby developing in her womb.

prey
Animals that are hunted for food by others (predators).

R

rorqual
A baleen whale with grooves in its throat. The grooves allow the throat to expand when the animal is taking in water when it is feeding.

S

school
Another name for a group of whales.

species
A particular kind of living thing. All living things of the same species look alike and can reproduce with one another.

splashguard
A raised area in front of the blowholes of some whales. It helps to prevent water from entering the blowholes when the whales breathe.

spout
Spout is another word for blow.

spy-hopping
Poking the head out of the water so that the eyes are above the surface.

stranding
Coming out of the water on to the shore and becoming stuck, or stranded.

streamlined
Shaped to slip through the water easily without much resistance.

T

tail fin
Another name for a whale's flukes.

temperate
A climate in which the weather is not too hot and not too cold.

toothed whale
A whale that has teeth rather than baleen plates in its mouth. Toothed whales include sperm whales, dolphins and porpoises.

tropical
The climate in the Tropics, the region on either side of the Equator, where the seas are always warm.

W

whale
A cetacean. Commonly the term is applied to the large whales, such as the baleen and sperm whales.

whalebone
A popular name for baleen, though baleen is not bone.

whaling
Hunting whales for their meat and blubber.